Online Dating For Women: The Basics

CASSIE LEIGH

TITLES BY CASSIE LEIGH

CONTENTS

INTRODUCTION

So you've decided to give online dating a try. Maybe a few of your friends found their spouses that way, or you're tired of the bar scene, or you're recently out of a long-term relationship and wouldn't even know where to go to find the bar scene, or maybe you want to tell your mom that you're making some sort of effort to meet someone without actually having to meet them.

Whatever the reason, you want to give this online dating thing a try. And, because we all hate rejection, you'd like to do it the "right way." Well, good on ya. I admire your starry-eyed optimism and resolve.

Unfortunately, you don't even know where to begin. What site should you choose? What should you say in your profile? Who should you avoid?

Hopefully this book will help you with all of that and more. Can you stumble through without it? Absolutely. You can get started online dating without spending a dime. Join a free site today and you'll be hearing from men within the hour.

But if you want to actually stick with it long enough to find what you're looking for, it's probably a good idea to think a few things through first.

I can't promise success—no one can—but I can at least help give you a good solid start.

Online dating requires healthy amounts of persistence, optimism, and an ability to shrug off the crazy shit your fellow humans will throw at you.

(Ah, the stories I could tell ...)

And luck. But you know the saying, the harder you work, the more luck you'll see. So let's get started and give you every advantage we can.

DISCLAIMER:
TARGET AUDIENCE

Before we go any further, I want to point out that this book is geared towards women. Like it or not, women's and men's online dating experiences are very different, and it turns out it's a lot simpler to focus on one group or the other rather than trying to go back and forth.

Also, in this context, we're talking about heterosexual women. I, quite frankly, don't have enough insight into the LGBT experience to do it justice from a dating advice perspective. While some of the chapters will be useful to anyone entering into online dating, I think it may fall apart after that. A woman dating a woman is not going to have the same issues as a woman dating a man.

And this is based on my experience online dating in the United States. If your country has a robust online dating culture, like the U.S., then what I say here will likely be true for your country as well. But having tried online dating in a smaller country with a less developed online dating culture, I can say that my experience there was very, very different than my experience in the U.S. So keep that in mind, too.

WHAT IS YOUR GOAL?

The first thing you have to do before anything else is determine why you're doing this, because your reasons for online dating are going to drive every other choice you make. This is just for you. Tell your friends or mom or grandma whatever you want, but be honest with yourself. Because what you want will drive everything from your user name to the site you use to who you choose to meet.

Are you looking for lasting love or just trying to find someone to hook up with for a little fun?

If you're just looking for a good time, this whole online dating thing is going to be much, much simpler for you than it is for the person trying to find "the one".

It will. People are people and there are plenty of men online looking for sex. If that's what you want too, and you're willing to be open about it, you'll find it. Now, I'm not saying you're going to end up with some hottie. If you want good looks AND sex, well, that's a much harder goal. Especially if you aren't amazingly good-looking yourself.

But if you just want sex with someone around your age and willing, it's pretty easy. Be honest about it and find the sites or apps that are known for that sort of thing.

If you want lifelong happiness with one special person, it's going to be much more challenging. Not impossible, just challenging. Online dating is still dating. And a lot of the issues that kept you from finding a partner in the real world are going to keep you from finding someone online, too. But at least with online dating you can see a much larger pool of potential mates and you get to do it at home in your pajamas or when you're standing in the checkout line at the grocery store.

If you're looking for something serious, don't get discouraged. You can find a life partner through online dating. I have multiple friends who are happily married to people they met online.

Just know that finding that special person to spend the rest of your life with will be far more challenging than finding someone to spend a night with—especially if you're someone with very high standards.

What I do know is that the women who are most successful at online dating are the ones who are persistent, open to meeting a wide variety of men, and flexible about what they're looking for.

And whether you find someone or not will also depend very much on what you're looking for. In my experience there are a lot of perfectly decent, nice men on these sites. They're not phenomenal men who leave you thinking, "I can't believe how cool and attractive this guy is." But they're solid, good-hearted, earnest types who want someone to spend their life with and will be good, reliable partners.

If that's what you want—a typical, stand-up kind of guy—I think you have a pretty good shot at finding him.

If you want more than that, well, that's going to be harder. (Just like in real life.) Hopefully not impossible. I mean, *you're* on there, right? And I'd assume that you're on a level with the type of guy you're looking for. Chances are if you're doing it a guy like you is, too. But maybe not as many as the good and solid types. It's going to take more of your time and effort if you want someone "special."

Honestly, if that's what you want and you haven't exhausted the friend-of-a-friend referrals and haven't yet approached that cute guy you see every week at rock climbing, I'd suggest doing that first before you wade into online dating. But if you've exhausted all your real world possibilities or like the idea of knowing a little bit about a guy before you let him chat you up, then online dating it is.

Okay, so back to the main point of the chapter: Why are you online dating? What do you want?

Sex?

Friendship?

A fuck buddy?

A steady Friday night date that doesn't care who your Saturday night is spent with?

A long-term, but not marriage-minded committed relationship?

Marriage?

Marriage and babies?

You can find any of the above. You just have to approach it the right way.

Step one is being honest with yourself about what you want. Step two is being honest with others about what you want. (And if you really aren't sure, like a friend of mine wasn't, choose one but be open to men that fall outside of that choice.)

PICKING A SITE OR APP:
STEP ONE – FREE OR PAID?

Now that you know what you want from online dating, it's time to pick a site or app.

Ah, choices.

There are so many sites or apps out there and they're changing all the time, so I'm not going to recommend specific ones. I'm just going to give you some general things to think about.

First, you need to decide whether to choose a paid site (like eHarmony or Match) or a free site (like OkCupid or Plenty of Fish).

In my experience, the ones that charge money generally attract more serious users. From what I've seen, the free sites tend to have more men that are less accomplished professionally, less skilled at communicating with a woman, and generally on the younger end of things (or recently divorced or separated).

That doesn't mean that there aren't great guys on the free sites. It just means that the signal to noise ratio is going to be much higher and you're going to have to wade through a lot more crap to find quality.

Free is cheap, but you pay for it in other ways.

If you're just looking to hook-up, go with the free sites. Hook-ups are easy. You put up a hot photo, message guys you find attractive, and things happen. Or you put up a hot photo and wade through the umpteen million one-liner responses you'll receive until you find a guy who looks interesting.

If you're looking for a serious relationship or marriage, then I say spend a little money. You'll be better able to hang in there long enough to find a good match.

How long should you plan for? My male and female friends who were really serious about finding someone generally managed to do so within ten weeks or so of joining the site. I honestly don't think you'll care to spend more than about three months on any one site before you decide to move on.

However, many of the sites offer ridiculous price discounts if you join for longer. The last site I joined cost $11 a month if you joined for a year or $40 a month if you joined for three months. (They do this because it makes it look like they have more members than they do. It also gives them more matches to send you even if the person they're sending you hasn't been online in six months.)

So if you join a paying site, plan for three months. Free is free, so no worries there.

PICKING A SITE OR APP:
STEP TWO – PRIVACY

Next you need to think about privacy. When you date in the real world, your dating life tends to stay separate from your professional life unless you deliberately let the two mix. Date your co-workers and your personal life becomes everyone's business. Get drunk with your co-workers and hook up with some random person at the bar while they're watching, that gets back to them, too. But spend your weekends at your neighborhood bar with your friends from high school and no one really cares or knows.

Online dating is different. First, some sites make your online dating profile public in order to attract other members. Is that okay for you? Are you comfortable with having your boss, co-workers, or other professional colleagues able to see your profile?

Some of these public sites ask about smoking, drug usage, sexual preference, sexual experience, etc. Would you feel comfortable answering those questions honestly knowing that anyone can see them? (If you don't answer honestly, what's the point? The people you meet on there are not going to be who you want to meet or you're not going to be who they want to meet.)

You still have to think about this with the subscription sites. I had a good buddy who was on Match for a long time and they kept suggesting the secretary in our office as a potential match for him. She could see what he said about himself and he could see what she said about herself. He could also see the photos she posted, which made for some interesting office gossip.

I once had a match that turned out to be a guy I went to high school with. Another time a site suggested a former co-worker as a potential match. Are you comfortable having the people in your life see your dating profile? Because if you're going to date online, it will happen.

Think about it now before you have to deal with it in the office on Monday morning or at Thanksgiving with the family.

The other privacy issue you need to consider is what the site reveals about you by the way it's structured.

I don't know of any sites that use your full name, but there are some that show your real first name to other users. (eHarmony, for example.) That's fine for people with names like Jane and Mike, but not so good for people with really unique names.

I have a friend with a unique enough name that you can use her first name and the city she lives in (which most of these sites also show) to find her home address and LinkedIn profile which lists her current employment and the schools she attended.

Maybe you don't think that's an issue. You think, "So what? What if your matches can find you in the real world?" If you like a guy, you're going to tell him those things eventually, right?

Here's the thing. Just like in real life, you will meet some crazy fucking people online dating. (On some days it seems like that's all there is.) Do you really want someone you've never met, who now maybe knows things about your personal and sexual preferences, showing up on your front doorstep because they can't understand why you shut down that match when you guys are clearly soul mates?

No? Then think carefully about what you're revealing about yourself and find a site that works within your comfort level.

(By the way, the way to solve this with eHarmony is to know about it when you sign up for your account and provide an initial or nickname when you list your name. As far as I know, once you put in your name it doesn't let you change it, so you have to get this right when you join.)

PICKING A SITE OR APP: STEP THREE – COMMUNICATION PREFERENCES

Okay. So, you're going to pick a site that aligns with your goals and gives you the privacy you need. Next you need to give some thought to how you like to communicate with people.

Some options (like eHarmony) have a structured communication approach. You get to ask three multiple-choice questions, then they answer, then they ask you three multiple-choice questions. Then you get to ask three open-ended questions, then they answer, and ask you three open-ended questions, then ...You get the point.

With those sites, your first few interactions are structured. It's good because it prevents the "hey, you" kind of e-mail that some men like to send. (Or scares those types of guys off completely.)

It's also good for someone who's nervous about communicating. You don't have to think of what to say—the site does it for you. It lets you ease into the whole thing. And, because it's structured and those early steps are designed to ferret out key differences, you can weed out bad matches early on.

I happen to be a TV Junkie and not all men like that. They put it on their list of traits they can't stand and I get to move on before it becomes an issue. Win-win.

I also use it to weed out the too-focused-on-sex types. If a man's ten must-have traits include sexually experienced, sensual, physically demonstrative, and physically fit, I close it down. Not because I'm anti-sex, but because the man still hasn't grown up enough to realize that there's more to a good relationship than being with a hot woman who wants to have sex with him.

So there are advantages to structured communication. But it can also kill the momentum, destroy any natural chemistry that exists between two people, or mask someone's social ineptitude.

(Also, keep in mind with eHarmony that if you choose to provide your own answer, saying "all of the above" or "A and C" are useless answers, because the person reading your answer can't see what your choices were.)

Back to the disadvantages of the structured approach.

Imagine meeting someone in real life. Instead of getting to just chat with them and let the conversation go where it will, you have to ask and respond to a set of structured questions that don't show your personality and don't let the other person show theirs.

"What are your must haves?"

"Well, I want a man who is kind, funny, and intelligent. What are your must haves?"

"I want a woman who is physically passionate, fit, and kind. What are your can't stands?"

"I don't like men who objectify women."

And so on and so forth. Yawn.

If you're looking for marriage and babies, maybe the structured approach is better. It lets you address some of those key issues before you get ahead of yourself. If you're looking for tonight's hook-up, it's a definite waste of time and energy.

If you want something serious there are sites that don't put you through that approach. Your best bet is to ask around. Do an internet search or two. Not for the sites, most don't tell you enough to make that determination, but for bloggers who review the sites. See what others have to say and decide if that approach will work for you.

PICKING A SITE OR APP:
STEP FOUR – LEVEL OF CONTROL

Okay, you've found a site that aligns with your goals, gives you the privacy you need, and lets you communicate in the way that works best for you.

What next?

Decide whether you want a site that will let you choose your own matches or one that's going to help you find the "right" match for you.

If you're looking for casual, you probably don't care too much about the "right" match. To be physically compatible you probably don't even have to like each other. (And now is not the time to digress into the "be careful who you sleep with because you may end up liking them so much you stay with them even though you hate a lot of things about them" lecture. Although, well, what I just said.)

If you're serious about finding a long-term relationship, it's possible that a site that chooses for you will help you get past certain biases you might have.

You know, like going for pretty blue eyes instead of common interests. Or only doctors and lawyers when the best fit for you is a self-employed graphic designer.

The benefits of a site that filters matches based upon your personality profile is that theoretically you're only focusing on all those other attributes after they've found you people who are compatible on the emotional/psychological level.

Theoretically.

Now, let's stop and discuss this for a minute.

I've tried a few of these sites and, in my experience, they don't always work as well as you'd like them to. Some, like OkCupid, allow the users to decide whether to use the matching algorithms. They tell each user the percent compatibility between them and their potential match, but you can contact anyone.

In my experience men rarely if ever let a low compatibility score keep them from reaching out to a woman they find attractive. And, since answering the questions that generate the compatibility numbers is optional, most just skip it, which means that even if it matters to you most men won't have answered enough questions for it to work.

What could be really helpful in narrowing down possible matches, isn't at all. Which is too bad because it's the only site I know of where you can have some pretty freaky preferences and use those matching algos to find other people with the same kinks. But it only works if people answer the questions and pay attention to the answers.

(Random aside. I said this book isn't for women seeking women, but a lesbian friend of mine tells me that OkCupid seems to be the best site for that. And know that certain sites, like eHarmony, don't even accept users who want same sex matches. They redirect you to a different site.)

Some sites, like eHarmony and Chemistry, force you to complete a questionnaire before you can join and then they do use the results to choose matches for you.

What about those sites?

Well, remember that whole discussion about how there are a lot of perfectly decent ordinary folks that do online dating? I think those sites work great for them.

Someone like me? Not so much.

This isn't arrogance talking (although I am arrogant). I'm just not normal.

I've taken the Myers-Briggs (MBTI) a few times and supposedly my personality type is present in less than 5% of the population. Which, given my experience on those sites, seems pretty accurate. That means that there are a very small number of men that are good fits for me.

If those sites only gave me that handful of matches that were truly compatible, that would be fine. I'd rather have a small number of matches that really work for me than ten a day. Instead, they give me lots of matches that just don't work.

Each time I've taken one of those questionnaires, the site nailed my personality profile and what I'm looking for. I'd read it and think, "Yes, this. This is me and what I want."

And then they'd give me men that didn't meet it.

I think part of the issue was that I was appealing to the men they matched me up with, but the men weren't appealing to me. On Chemistry I was an Explorer personality and all the, I think it was Builders, found me really interesting, because I'd traveled and done things. I found them boring, because they hadn't.

If you have a unique personality type, expect some disappointment even with the personality matching sites.

So what do you do if you are one of those unique personalities? Is it better to avoid the personality matching sites?

Maybe. Problem is there aren't going to be more people like you on the other sites. (Unless people with your personality type tend to choose the same kind of parameters so go for the same types of sites in which case just follow you gut about what you like the best.)

At least with the personality matching sites you have a snowball's chance in hell of getting a good match. On the other sites, the haystack you're searching through is even bigger and the chance of finding that needle (i.e. match) are really small.

Again, this is assuming what you want is long-term. Short-term, who cares?

Bottom line? Unique personalities need to be prepared to

be frustrated by a lack of appealing choices and need to force themselves to stick with it longer than normal folks.

Back to the basic question: use a site that picks matches for you or use a site that lets you pick your own matches?

If you choose one of the sites where it's a free-for-all, as a woman you may be at a disadvantage depending on how stereotypically attractive you are.

Doubt me? What criteria do you think men search by first? Age. Height. Eye color. Hair color. Body type.

They're men and I mean them no insult when I say that most men, or at least those men's friends, put a premium on physical looks. It matters to them, and when given the opportunity to search for women based upon those criteria, they will.

There's also such a thing as choice overload. I won't link to some boring psychology study, but one or more do exist that basically say that having too many choices is worse than having a limited number of choices. If you can only have A, B, or C, you're pretty happy when you get B. If you can have A-Z, then you're comparing B to everything else you could have had and feel less satisfied.

Limited choices help result in long-term relationships.

Women can also fall into the trap of looking for all the wrong things on those sites too. (Assuming again, that we're talking about serious relationships.) If you use a site where you get to find matches and you put income and education at the top of your list, you may end up dating a few douchebags with nothing else going for them and missing some really great guys that you might have liked if you'd gone with a site that chooses for you.

One last thought. For me the anyone-can-contact-anyone sites are a little overwhelming. Because anyone can message you. And they do. Being vain, I put up a good photo, and get far too many responses to handle, most from men that aren't at all a good fit for me. YMMV.

AN ASIDE: PEOPLE LIE

You have to be careful with online dating because people lie. Many profiles are what you might call aspirational rather than realistic.

If you honestly think that searching for six foot or taller men with incomes of over $100K is going to find you those men, I'd like to sell you some ocean-front property in Arizona. There might be a few in there. But there'll be a lot of 5'10" guys who earn $60K but hope you won't notice the height difference and know you won't be able to tell the income difference right away.

And be careful of anyone whose age is listed as 29, 39, or 49. They could very well be 30, 40, or 50 and just be lying so they can appear in the lower age bracket searches.

Just like in the real world, people are insecure and most aren't comfortable with who they are. (Don't be one of those people, by the way. Just because others lie doesn't mean you should.)

Always proceed with caution.

PICKING A SITE OR APP: STEP FIVE – SPECIALTY SITE OR POPULAR SITE?

Alright. So that's the basics.

One, find a site that aligns with your goals.

Two, find one that gives you the privacy you need.

Three, find one that lets you communicate in the way that works best for you.

Four, find one that provides you with the right tools to help find the person you're looking for.

What else?

What about those specialty sites. Should you use them?

Maybe. But remember that the more niche the site, the smaller the population of potential matches. Which is fine if the focus of the site matters to you enough or if that helps you narrow down your choices to a really great population of possibles. But don't assume that it'll work that way.

Let me give you an example.

I recently found an online dating site where you could post about books you liked and find other singles that liked the same books. Perfect for someone like me. I'm a voracious reader and I believe you can tell a helluva lot about someone by what they like to read.

So I checked out the site. There were a ton of men on there who had experienced life-changing transformations after reading *Outliers* by Malcolm Gladwell. Me? I hated that book. I thought the guy covered really interesting topics and then drew poor conclusions based upon unsubstantiated facts. I swore to never read another book by him which meant I certainly had no interest in dating any man who thought it was the best book he'd ever read.

Interesting site, but obviously not for me. It didn't attract my type of guy. Which is when I realized that, as much as I love to read, most of the men I've really clicked with over the years haven't been big readers. Whatever it is that connects me to the men I like, it's not their ability to discuss the latest bestseller. As a matter of fact, there's no way to kill my mood faster than to have some guy spout off about a book I really liked, because it's rare for me to talk to someone about a book I liked or disliked and have us agree on the details of why we liked or disliked it.

Another example is a site for dog lovers. I love my dog and it would make life so much easier if I could find someone who wanted to hang out at the dog park on weekends or understands why I don't want to leave my dog alone just to go have dinner with a stranger.

But there are different types of dog lovers. I take my pup to the lake to swim and let her roll in the mud. She generally has a handful of leaves tangled in her coat. Well, a dog-lover site full of men who dressed their Shih-Tzus in pink dresses and went to dog shows wouldn't work for me.

So do your homework before you choose a specialty site. And make sure there are enough choices on there to make it worth your time. If you can, look at some actual profiles before you take the plunge.

I will say that if you're religious-minded, it's probably a very good idea to use one of the sites focused on your religion, because shared religious views help form a stable long-term relationship and most of those sites have enough users to be worthwhile. As a non-religious person, I can say that people like me will usually avoid the religious sites, so you're not going to find yourself really liking someone who doesn't share the same fundamental beliefs as you if you stick with one of those sites.

PICKING A SITE OR APP: STEP SIX – HOW MANY TO START WITH?

Just choose one at first. Seriously. Trust me on this. You just need one to start out. If you don't like it, you can always join another later.

I had a friend do eHarmony and Match on her first attempt at online dating. It was overwhelming.

We'll talk more about this later, but most women get a lot of attention when they join up. My friend ended up focusing almost exclusively on eHarmony and even that was a lot for her to juggle.

She was very positive about the whole thing, so willing to meet any of her matches that wanted to meet her and willing to approach men who hadn't messaged her. Those first few weeks she went on about six dates a week. Just from eHarmony.

She met someone after about ten weeks, but I think part of the reason she went with him was burnout from so much attention on all the sites.

Here's the deal: As a woman on these sites, you are going to end up rejecting more men than you probably ever have in your life. It's not fun. It's not enjoyable to not want to respond to a message from some perfectly nice guy who just doesn't interest you at all. It drags on you. Well, it drags on me. It's the worst part of online dating in my opinion.

Pace yourself when you start out. One site only. Add as needed.

PICKING A SITE OR APP: STEP SEVEN – CAN YOU TURN IT OFF?

Another thing to consider: Can you stop the site from sending you new matches? I joined a site, Chemistry, a number of years ago. Without even posting a photo, I had twenty-plus matches by the next morning. I wanted to turn off new matches while I worked my way through the first batch, but found I wasn't able to. The only way to turn off new matches was to turn off all matches.

I did not last long on that site. My mother raised me to be polite and simply ignoring ten or fifteen men a day stressed me out beyond belief. But I was also unwilling to spend my entire evening communicating with them just to keep up.

(Maybe they've fixed that issue by now—it was a while ago. Just be careful.)

Also, think long and hard before you join a site that won't let you hide the fact that you're online. There are a few, like OkCupid, that seem to send out a special alert when you log on so that men who are just sitting there waiting for fresh meat can start bombarding you with messages like "Hey there" and "What's up?"

If you like that sort of thing, then go for it. If you know that getting meaningless messages from guys who didn't do anything more than glance at your profile photo and decide they'd be happy to do you, then skip that site.

(With OkCupid you can pay for the privilege to hide that information, but that just seems offensive to me somehow. I have to pay them to not be harassed by the men I'm supposed to want to date? No thanks.)

Almost all sites do let other users see the last time you logged on. And some will show the last time you viewed that person's profile. For me, that's one of the most annoying aspects of many of the sites. It's my business when I go on there and what I look at, but the sites make money by providing that type of information, so you can't really get around it.

One hint: For the free sites that make profiles public, you can go to the site without logging on and check out profiles that might interest you that way. Keeps you from getting contacted by the vultures that are just waiting for a live woman to log on to the site and lets you check someone out without the site notifying them.

TIME TO TAKE A BREATHER AND SUMMARIZE

There's a lot to consider, but you probably aren't going to go wrong if you stick with the big sites.

Honestly, if it's too much just try Match your first time out the gate. To me it feels a lot like the world's biggest pickup bar except without the ability to limit it to one guy at a time offering to buy you a drink, but it's the all-purpose site with enough members for everyone.

If you want casual, I hear Tinder or AdultFriendFinder work well. I would also put OkCupid or Plenty of Fish in that category.

For serious I would say eHarmony and, although I've never used them since I lack strong religious beliefs, Christian Mingle or JDate.

With all sites, here are the key things to keep in mind:

1. Pick a site that aligns with what you want. Free is more likely to be casual, paid is more likely to be serious.

2. Pick a site that meets your privacy needs while realizing that you probably cannot maintain your privacy completely.

3. Only pick a specialty site if you're really, truly passionate about that particular niche and you can see that the type of

people on that site are passionate about it in the same way you are.

4. Choose a site that matches how you like to communicate.

5. Choose a site that will give you the right tools to meet someone and, if you have a unique personality type, be prepared for any personality matching algorithms to not be as effective for you as they are for others.

6. Do your homework. Ask friends what worked for them. Find out how a site works before you join it.

7. Avoid sites where you can't turn off new matches.

8. Think long and hard before joining a site that tells other users when you're online.

9. Remember that people lie and don't assume that they really meet your criteria just because their profile says they do.

That's about it for finding a site. Next, what to do once you find one.

PICKING A USER NAME

Now that you've found a site, you need to think about how you're going to present yourself.

Not every site requires user names, but a lot of them do. And Partygirl22 is going to get a much different response than SuzieQ or Beachgirl.

So, who are you? And how do you want potential matches to see you?

Think about your goals in doing this. Women and men's experience of online dating is very different. Just as women and men's experience of dating in general is different. Women will be contacted and pursued more than men. It's just the way it goes.

Which means you will get contacted by men no matter what user name you choose. That makes it a little hard to know when you've chosen the wrong one. It may not be that the site doesn't have the type of guy you want. It may be that your user name (and photos and profile) are attracting the wrong type of guy.

If you're looking for sex or hook-ups or someone to party with then by all means choose a user name like that. Partygirl22, FunAndFlirty, something with the number 69 in it. Any of those will work. Subtlety is not needed.

But if you actually want a long-term relationship then avoid that shit. Attention $=/=$ serious interest. There is a difference between attracting attention and attracting the right kind of attention. With user names like the ones above, most women will receive responses, but they'll be from guys who are looking to party.

Worse yet, a lot of the serious-minded guys will look at that user name and move on to the next girl. Because BJ69 is not the future mother of his children no matter how often she volunteers to help the homeless.

Remember, the goal is to find someone who meets your needs.

Pick a name you can live with, that showcases your personality in some way or that is carefully neutral in a non-boring way, and, unless you really are just looking for sex, avoid the overtly sexual user names.

Also, if you are on a website that uses real names, like eHarmony, and you have a unique name then consider listing an initial, nickname, or more common abbreviation of your name that won't be so easy to Google.

THE DIFFERENCE BETWEEN
SEXY AND ATTRACTIVE

We just touched on it a bit, so now is probably the time to discuss the fact that there is a difference between being sexy and being attractive. Some women just naturally know where that line is. If you're one of those women, then skip this chapter.

But some women, especially younger ones (myself included when I was young), don't realize that there's a difference and they end up portraying themselves as sexy when what they really wanted to do was be attractive.

Why does this matter in online dating?

I think men have this switch in their minds and when it gets flipped over to the "she's sexy" setting a few key things go out the window. Like trying to get to know you, figuring out whether you have long-term compatibility, and respecting you in the workplace. If the sexy switch is flipped, a man focuses on having sex with you (or imagining having sex with you) and not much else.

That means that when it comes to dating he'll gloss over any differences you have that can interfere with that. Like how you refuse to date a smoker and he smokes every time he drinks. He'll figure he can get you in the sack before you figure that out. It's worth a try.

Some men, the worst of the worst, will outright lie to you to get you into bed. Others, more well-meaning but not immune to the sexy switch, will just fail to disagree with or correct you until after they've slept with you. That's always fun. All those sex chemicals raging through your blood and you start to finally see what the guy is really like.

Not good.

Even if you're just attractive to a man (not sexy), you can still run into this, but it's not near as blatant as when you flip the sexy switch in a guy's head.

Okay, so what's the difference between sexy and attractive. How do you draw the line?

That depends.

Great answer, huh? But it's true. If I were hanging on the Jersey Shore for the summer, I could get away with far more outrageous looks or behavior before I crossed that line. If I were in a conservative Connecticut enclave for the summer, it would take next to nothing to cross it. One bright, low-cut top and some short shorts and bam, I'd be "casual summer fling that never meets Mom." Of course, that also brings up the issue of trashy versus not, which is also context-specific and a whole other can of worms.

How do you know where you are on the sexy vs. attractive spectrum?

Ask your guy friends. Say, "If you saw this photo online dating, what would you think?"

And avoid the obvious triggers. Users names with the number 69 or a sexual pun are going to push you into sexy territory. A heel higher than three inches, a cleavage shot that shows more than 50% of your boobs, licking your lips provocatively, a picture that seems to look up a short skirt …Any of those will be flip the sexy switch.

Unless, of course, what you're looking for is short-term. Then do all of the above.

But if you want to get to something serious, dial it back

enough to get there. Better to receive a few responses that are legitimate than lots of responses that have no interest in you as a person.

We'll talk later about certain women who actually need to dial it up a notch, but that's for later.

PICKING YOUR PROFILE PHOTOS

The next step is to pick your profile photos. This is especially important for women. All men will look at your photos; only about half of men will read much of your profile. Men are visual creatures. It's just the way they are.

A July 2014 blog post on the OkCupid blog even implies that your picture is ALL that matters. I'd hedge that a bit and say that for OkCupid users that's probably true. I happen to know a few folks that clearly do not value looks in their relationships and those people do not go to OkCupid when they choose a dating site.

My completely unscientific, observation-based opinion would be this: In general, men value looks far more than women and any woman on any online dating site should take that into serious consideration when she posts her photos. This is based upon my own personal experience with men and with observing my male and female friends.

Now, first step (again) is determining what you want from online dating.

Are you looking for a hot hookup? Choose photos that indicate that you'd be a good choice for that.

What does that mean? If I were only looking for sex, I wouldn't bother posting any sort of professionally-taken photos unless those photos were from a Victoria's Secret ad. No corporate headshots. (Well, for any type of dating really...)

If you want casual, keep your photos casual. For women, it's pretty easy. Selfies that show your boobs are a good start. Lots of smiling. Makeup beats no makeup. Post full body photos, preferably with little to no clothing.

Seriously. If it sounds like I'm advising you to make your profile look like it came out of Playboy, it's because I am. There's a reason those kinds of magazines sell as well as they do. Men are visual and if you want to attract their *sexual* interest you need to play to that.

Now, if you want something more serious and long-term, then you need to think long and hard before posting too many "fun" photos of yourself. If you want a man to see you as a potential spouse and mother of his children, you probably don't want to post a photo of yourself doing a kegstand, no matter how flattering the photo might be.

If you want serious, find photos that show your interests and make you look attractive but are not overly sexy. Recommendations from some of my guy friends include photos of you doing outdoorsy activities or traveling. As they say on OkCupid, "If you want worthwhile messages in your inbox, the value of being conversation-worthy, as opposed to merely sexy, cannot be overstated."

You also need to think about the type of person you're trying to attract. If you want someone active and outdoorsy, then post active and outdoorsy photos of yourself. If you want someone who goes to wine tastings and art exhibits, then post photos of yourself in more sophisticated outfits or settings— wearing a little black dress and sipping a glass of wine, for example.

I would recommend being careful with including alcohol in your photos, though. One photo with alcohol is fine. Every photo with alcohol implies that you might have a drinking problem.

And, no matter how good that photo of you with your ex was, don't use it. It's obvious when you're all dressed up and you cut off half of the photo that you must be posting a photo with an ex.

Also be careful of photos of you and one guy. If you decide to use one of those, be very clear in the photo description who that guy is. And then step back and figure out how creepy it is for you to post a photo of yourself with that guy on your dating profile.

(I had a match post about four photos of himself with his sister. It was just odd to me. So, know you're being judged and plan accordingly.)

Personally, I also avoid group shots. One, sometimes it comes off looking too party-like, which tips things back into the "just having a good time" category. Two, the other people in that photo don't necessarily need their photo up on a dating site. And, three, if that's all you post, your potential matches may not even know which one is you.

Your photos should also be current. Nothing more than a year or two old. I know, I know, you looked so good ten years ago at your best friend's wedding. But, they're not going to date the you of ten years ago. They're dating who you are right now, so show them what they're getting. Nothing worse than showing up for a date and being severely disappointed by what you find because the person lied.

And, this should go without saying, post photos of yourself, not someone else. (I had a date tell me some woman used photos of her sister. WTF? What is someone hoping to achieve by doing that? You do want to meet this person in real life, right? Well, think that through…)

You should also think about the quality of the photos you post. Personally, I think professionally-taken photos stand out like a sore thumb, but the nicer the photo, the better you look. Use a high-resolution camera instead of a crappy phone, avoid harsh lighting, and make sure you're the focus of the photo. (There's another OkCupid blog that discusses this in far more detail.)

So, here's what I recommend whether you're looking for casual or serious:

1. Your main photo should be a close-up shot of your face.

2. It should be a smiling photo, making eye contact with the camera, and looking a little flirty or, at a minimum, friendly and open to a conversation.

3. You should have more than one photo posted and at least one should be a full body shot. (I know men who won't even message a woman unless they can see her full body and I've had men message me and ask me to post one when I didn't have one up.)

4. Current photos only unless you make it clear that it's an older photo and it's up there to prompt conversation.

5. If you're going to break from the above, make sure you're doing something to trigger people's interest so they'll communicate with you.

6. Post photos that will appeal to the type of person you're looking to meet. (And that legitimately reflect your interests. If you want someone outdoorsy, you should probably be outdoorsy too.)

7. Post quality photos taken under good lighting with a good camera and where you're the focus of attention.

BE A WOMAN NOT A PROFESSIONAL

Before we continue, I think it's time for a brief pause to talk about a problem that some women face. And that's the inability to turn off their business persona when they start dating.

I will tell you this now: Unless you're in a career that rewards a woman for being womanly, what makes you successful in your professional career will interfere with your ability to be successful at dating.

I watched *The Singles Project* and there was a woman on there who is a very beautiful and accomplished professional. In the first episode, she had to ask a guy for his number and then call him back to set up a date. He said no. Why? Because she spoke to him like she was arranging a job interview.

She called him up, got right to the point, and was very precise with her words and terse in her speech. There wasn't an ounce of warmth or flirtation in her voice. Men don't react well to that. Being clear and concise is an incredibly valuable skill in certain business professions, but it will fail you in a dating context.

What makes you appealing in your professional life doesn't necessarily make you an attractive mate. Harsh, but true.

As an example:

I went to a very good university. If I were a man, I'd say

that I went to that school and the woman across the table from me would lean in a little closer, smiling, and say, "Oh, really?"

But I'm not a man, I'm a woman. And the standard male reaction is to sit back a little bit, look slightly uncomfortable, and say, "Oh. You must be smart."

If I add what I majored in and that I have an MBA, the conversation is usually over at that point. Granted, the last time this conversation occurred it was with a guy who'd failed out of community college three times and worked as a parking lot attendant, so maybe there was a reason that it killed the conversation.

Point is, as a woman, many of the non-dating things that you consider successes get in the way of you meeting a man. It takes a special man to hear those kinds of "qualifications", know he doesn't have anything approaching them, and still think he has a shot.

If you are a highly accomplished woman, odds are you'll be dating men that are not as accomplished as you. That doesn't mean you get to sit back and say you'll never find a man because all men are intimidated by you. (The right man won't be.) It does mean that you need to step back and remember that you're dating not trying to get a promotion.

You need to sell yourself (figuratively not literally) to a man as a warm and supportive partner and companion.

DO NOT treat your dating profile like a resume. Do not list your academic achievements. Do not brag about your job and how you're the youngest whatever or that you're an SVP at a Fortune 500 company.

I know. Writing those words makes me cringe. You worked hard for what you've achieved and your proud of it and want to be with a man who values you for who you are and can accept that you're successful.

I agree. And I'm not telling you to lie about it or hide anything about yourself. All I'm saying is remember that most men aren't going to be attracted to you for those traits.

You will find a man who can take it all in stride, but not by shoving your accomplishments in his face on day one.

Think of it this way: He's looking for someone he can come home to at the end of the day. Someone to eat dinner with and spend an enjoyable evening with. What does that woman look like? Does all of her conversation revolve around herself and her achievements? No. She's warm, can have a great conversation about his interests, likes to laugh, and can cook an amazing manicotti.

I'm sure many of your friends are as accomplished as you are. Do you like them because of their professional accomplishments? No. Hell, I'm not even sure what my best friend's job title even is. So focus on the personal and leave the professional at the door.

I'm not saying to lie—I once actually had a guy I knew suggest that I should. I think that's bullshit and I'd never do it and I don't recommend that you do. (Unless you're looking for something casual, in which case do whatever you want.)

No, you still need to be who you are, you just need to focus on showing the man you like that you're the type of woman he wants to date. If he wants someone sophisticated and accomplished talk about your interest in opera or classical music or how you play in the city orchestra once a month. If he wants outdoorsy, talk about how you like to take hikes or travel. (Only if those things are actually true.)

Connect with him as a woman—as the person you are when you aren't at work. And if you don't know who that is because all you do is work, get out there and enjoy some down time before you try to meet someone.

FILLING OUT YOUR PROFILE:
PART ONE – WHAT TO SAY

Alright, so you have a site and photos, now it's time to say something about yourself.

Let's eliminate the easy one first. If you want something casual, then you don't need to say much. Just that you're looking to have a good time and like to party. If your pictures and profile name support it, that's about all you have to do.

You could talk about exactly what you will or won't do or the kind of guy you'll do it with, but, honestly, men aren't going to pay much attention to that. They'll just message you based upon user name and photo. Weed out the ones you don't want after they message you and go from there.

For those who want something serious, it's a little trickier.

No matter what you do, you're going to have to wade through responses from guys who didn't read your profile and just took a shot. Or guys who did read your profile and decided they'd write you even though they're not what you're looking for.

As an example, I put in my profile that I don't like smokers. Casual, daily, I don't care. I hate cigarette and cigar smoke and want nothing to do with it. I still get messages from men who smoke. Some say they do and ask why I won't give them a shot. Some don't mention it but have profile photos of themselves smoking.

I have yet to find a way to limit the responses I receive to men that actually fit my criteria. Spelling it out doesn't work because on every site men are given the ability to ignore your preferences.

So you can say a lot or say a little and it may not even matter.

If you do put in a lot, I'd try to include things that will spark conversation. And I think demonstrating a sense of humor is always a good thing.

I would also suggest that you keep it positive. Because, again, if we're thinking about who a guy wants to come home to at the end of the day it's probably not Negative Nellie. Even if you don't keep it positive, you'll probably still get responses from men if you have an attractive photo. Just know that you might be scaring off the better possibilities with your negativity.

(Although, I will admit I tend to be pretty snarky in my profiles. It's the only way to keep things manageable for me. It's either find a way to limit my options or drop off entirely.)

I've seen some people advise that you don't put too much text, because men don't like that. Personally, I say be yourself. If you like to put a lot of text in your profile, put a lot of text. But don't feel like you have to. Short and sweet will work too.

Just know that the more text you put, the less likely your matches will read all of it.

If you're given a chance to list favorite movies, TV shows, or music think about using it as an opportunity to show a unique side of your personality. It's great to like *Scandal,* but maybe more interesting to list some obscure BBC show instead. If the guy knows it, it's an instant conversation starter. *Scandal?* Well, you're like ten profiles he just looked at.

And, remember, privacy. Don't put things in your profile that will let someone track you down in real life. Be generic rather than specific. I wouldn't post a photo of your home or talk about where you like to go hiking. Protect yourself for now. All these guys are still strangers to you.

Bottom line? You're a woman and the odds are in your favor here. Slap up some words and you'll likely get responses. Sadly, the photo is what matters the most for attracting interest.

FILLING OUT YOUR PROFILE: PART TWO – CATEGORIZING YOURSELF

All sites want to categorize their users. Some of those choices make a lot of sense. Are you male or female? Are you looking for someone who is male or female? Those types of questions are necessary and easy to answer for 99% of the population.

But most sites go past that. What is your religion? What is your ethnicity? What is your income? What is your education? What is your star sign?

Not only that, but how do you want your potential mate to answer those questions? And how important is it that they answer that way?

Not so easy anymore is it?

Well, let's talk about a few of those.

RELIGION

This is a very easy question to answer if you have a clear-cut religious belief. One of my very good friends is Jewish and there was no doubt in her mind when she went looking for a husband that he needed to be Jewish as well. A good friend of my brother's is also Jewish. He ended up marrying a non-religious woman from Taiwan who converted to Judaism to please the parents. I recently went on a date with a guy who listed himself as spiritual but not religious even though he grew up Jewish.

For someone like my friend, filling out those questions is easy. You say you're Jewish and that you want someone who is also Jewish. (Or, better yet, if you're like my friend, do what she did and put all of your mother's and grandmother's friends to work rooting out every single Jewish man they know and skip online dating altogether.)

For someone like my brother's friend or the guy I dated, it's more complicated. If you're religious but not strongly enough to care whether your partner is, or strongly enough for it to impact your lives together, do you list it? It matters to some, it doesn't matter to others. If you list yourself as a certain religion and then end up with matches who were looking for that religion, are they going to be disappointed by your level of observance?

I was raised Christian, but only go to church for weddings and funerals (and try to avoid both as much as possible), but I'm also not a fan of people who are openly atheist because I think it's a bit arrogant to assume that you can firmly conclude that there isn't a higher power. But I'm also not spiritual in the sense that I feel there's some spiritual energy connecting all of us. So for me, there's never a good category to choose.

What am I? Other? Not religious? Spiritual? What I end up picking depends on my mood at the time.

And I keep that in mind when I'm setting parameters for what type of mate I'd be willing to accept. There might be a not-very-Christian man who chooses Christian who could be my perfect match. Or maybe it's the spiritual but not religious guy. The wider the net you cast, the more choices you get. But the more mismatches as well.

If you do choose certain religions as acceptable and you aren't that religious, be alert to signs that the other person is very much a believer in the religion they've listed and be clear as soon as possible that you are not.

ETHNICITY

This is another fun one. I tend to approach this one from the "what do people see" perspective. Look at my photo and you see a white woman. You don't think mixed or multi-ethnic, you just think white. Truth of the matter is I have all sorts of different ethnic groups flowing through my veins. But I don't think that's what potential mates care about. I think they care about the woman they'll be seeing every day and introducing to their friends and family.

I also think they care about background and cultural traditions. My upbringing was also very white. Sure, we had more Christmas dinners that were Mexican food instead of ham or whatever it is normal white people have for Christmas, but all in all my upbringing was standard white-person upbringing.

So that's what I choose. And then I keep an eye out for someone who really, really wanted someone white. In the areas where I've lived, that's never been an actual issue, but it could be, so be aware of what the person you're with says.

In terms of who you want as a match, well, that's up to you. I had a friend who threw the net very wide and was open to any ethnicity. She really hit it off with a guy who was from a very different ethnic background than her. Seemed to work. Except when she thought long-term. Then she wondered what would happen when they had kids because they wouldn't look like her.

Gut check moment. I'm sure one or two people reading that just flinched. But it's a valid issue for some people and you need to know if it's one for you.

Now, maybe my friend would've grown past that little moment of whatever you want to call it. But I think it's better to think these things through before someone's heart is on the line.

Ask yourself: Would I be comfortable being seen in public as part of a couple with someone of this ethnicity? Would I be comfortable introducing someone of this ethnicity to my family? To my friends? Would I be comfortable having a child that was half this ethnicity? How would my family react to my dating someone of this ethnicity?

Ugly questions to ask yourself in this PC world of ours, but valid ones. Many people are fine being friends with members of different ethnic groups. But marrying someone of a different ethnicity? Well, not everyone is there yet. If you're not, don't waste your time or the other person's by pretending that you are.

AGE RANGE

Men are the funniest on this one. I've seen multiple men that list the age range they're looking for as anywhere from two years younger to twenty years younger than them. Haha. They wish.

I would take any age range you think is acceptable and expand it just a bit. Personally, I'm far more accomplished than most men my age, so I find it difficult to view younger men as equals that I would want to date, but I have to leave room for the possibility that there will be that exception to the rule.

And be honest about your own age. I know, it's tough, especially if you don't look your age. I'm close to forty and still get carded for beer almost everywhere. But it is what it is and you don't want to start a relationship off with lies. At a bar you can just not answer the question. Online it's mandatory and one of the first facts that the sites provide about you.

Another thing to consider is that your age is about more than your appearance. It's about your cultural references—I grew up on G.I. Joe and Strawberry Shortcake. A girl five to ten years younger than me probably didn't. And it's about where you are in life. Especially for women, there's a big difference between dating at twenty-eight and at thirty-eight. You're in a different place in your life than you were ten years ago. Accept that and own it.

INCOME

I don't know why any site asks this question. I find it offensive. And one I just joined doesn't even let you refuse to answer. Do they honestly think most men are honest about this? I doubt it. If they're going to lie about their age and height (and some definitely do), chances are they'll lie about this, too. So, don't rely on it to find matches.

Now, in terms of what to list for yourself. For most people, this will be easy. You have a salary and maybe a bonus and they come out to around $X every year. For someone who is self-employed, like myself, it's a helluva lot harder. The income I earned this year is five times the income I earned last year and half the income I earned five years ago. And next year, unless I change something in my current plan, I may earn next to nothing.

What number should someone like me choose? I went with the number most representative of my professional experience and place in life. A number that I have earned and that is comparable to what I would earn if I accepted a salaried position tomorrow.

I could've gone higher, but it would've been a stretch to do so. I would encourage you to choose an honest number that is in line with what you have earned and may earn again and to tip towards a higher number if you're right on the edge of a range.

And, when searching for matches, don't expect this to be accurate.

EDUCATION

This one's very straight-forward in terms of what you list. Either you have a degree or you don't. (And three credits shy of a degree is not having a degree. Honestly, if I were looking for a match I'd be far more judgmental of the person who stopped three credits shy of graduating but put down that they had a degree than I would be of the person who never went.)

What's tricky on this one is what you put down for a potential mate. I have a Master's degree from a very good school and an undergraduate degree from another very good school. And I can say quite comfortably that I'd rather date a self-starting entrepreneurial type that dropped out of state college to start his own business than someone with two PhDs who has never actually worked in his life.

If you're tempted to weigh this one heavily, ask yourself, why does his education matter to you? Do you see it as a proxy for achievement, because it's not. I know a number of men I went to school with at those fancy schools who are not accomplished. And I know a number of men who never went to college who are. Also, unless you can specify which schools someone attended, the criteria is virtually meaningless. Is an MBA from Harvard (definitely not one of my schools-ugh) equivalent to an MBA from the local community college? Absolutely not. Not at all.

And yet, if you list education as highly important or insist on only meeting matches with advanced degrees you're going to end up with matches like that and miss out on the guys who've succeeded at a less traditional path.

I say ignore education. Unless, of course, you come from one of those families or social groups where people have to have certain credentials in order to be accepted. If that's the case, I think you should skip online dating and use friends-of-friends or a matchmaker to meet someone because those groups look for far more than just the degree.

STAR SIGN

Should you use bizarre criteria to look for a mate? You know, like star sign?

I'm a rational, practical person and that side of my personality says, "Hell, no." But I have this great book that tells you how compatible you are with someone based upon the week of your birth and the week of their birth that has yet to be wrong.

So do as you will, but if some guy comes along and you feel "it" don't pass him by just because he's a Gemini.

TIME TO COMMUNICATE

So, you're ready to go. You've posted the photos and completed your profile. Time to let 'er rip.

If you're looking for casual, you're probably already out on a date somewhere, so we'll skip you. (Okay, fine. Maybe you need a hint or two. Be nice, be open to meeting up, keep the conversation low-key and casual, and don't insult the guy unless you're doing it to flirt.)

If you're in this for something more serious, here's what your first day might very well look like:

You decided to join one of those free sites and loaded everything to the site after work on Thursday, closed it down, and went to bed. You said you're interested in a long-term relationship and open to the possibility of marriage and kids.

The next morning you wake up to a notice that you have twenty-two new messages. Twenty-two! Wow.

This isn't matches we're talking about, but messages. You have even more matches than that, they just haven't written yet.

One of these guys has to be promising, right?

Sure. Why not.

You open the first one.

It's from a guy who explains that he's married and staying in the relationship for the kids. He complains that his wife won't have sex with him anymore, so he's joined the site looking for someone to sleep with on the side. He really likes your picture and you seemed nice.

He, of course, doesn't have a picture on his profile because he doesn't want anyone to know what he's up to, but he's happy to send a picture along privately if you're interested.

Off to a great start, aren't we?

The next message says, "Hey hottie! Whatcha up to tonight?" It was sent about a minute after you uploaded your photo. (The girls looking for something casual saw that message last night, responded, and hooked up an hour or two later.)

Message three sounds kind of good until you realize it's a cut and paste that the guy sends every woman that interests him. "My name is John and I am thirty-two. I like long walks and am looking for a woman to walk with me through life."

The next seven messages are more one-liners or cut and paste jobs.

By this time you're tempted to break out the vodka to numb the pain even though it's only nine in the morning. You find yourself fondly reminiscing about that creepy frat guy who cornered you at that party in college and wondering if you could track him down through the alum site. He hadn't really been that bad, had he? Hell, he's probably a successful hedge fund trader by now.

Message eleven is another with no profile picture. This one from a guy asking if you're into younger men.

Message twelve is from a man about twenty years older than you who is looking for someone to have great sex with. His profile picture shows him with a deep tan and a very large boat and you can tell that he thinks his honesty is refreshing.

Message thirteen is a long e-mail from a man explaining how much he likes to please women and how he's looking for someone to take a firm hand with him.

While you've been on the site reading the first batch of e-mails, you can see more men checking out your profile. The notices pile on top of each other in the corner like some sort of zombie attack.

By the time you're done with message fourteen, you already have five new messages—all of the "Hey sexy—what's up?" variety.

Nineteen messages down and you already want to close down your account and start searching the Internet for nunneries that don't require a strong religious vocation.

But message twenty looks promising. He's the right age, his profile doesn't include any deal-breakers, he's pretty cute (look at those eyes), and his message to you actually references something you said in your profile.

Congratulations, you're on your way.

(You think I'm joking with this, don't you? But as I just re-read that, I remembered every single message I received that prompted those descriptions. None of that is made up. And I didn't even include the guy who wanted me to have his kids in that list. It can get ugly out there. Be prepared and don't give up.)

Now, it might be tempting to message the one-liner or the cut and paste guys. Some of them are cute and have interesting profiles. I did it when I first started out and I won't blame you if you do it too. But chances are it's a waste of your time.

The one-liner guys are looking for something quick and casual. They want to meet up right now or have flirty chat conversation, but they're not willing to communicate back and forth until you're comfortable with them. All they went by was your photo, which isn't going to help you find anything real and lasting.

The cut and paste guys fall into one of two categories. There's the nervous guy who's never done this before and had his friends help him craft the perfect introductory message to send so he'd make a good first impression.

He means well, but the fact that he couldn't write something spontaneous that responded to your profile is not a good sign. He might be good at taking direction and doing exactly what you want, but he probably won't be able to anticipate your needs very well.

Now, if you like a good project, then maybe that's okay

with you. But if you want a guy who has the basics of interacting with women down, I'd say skip him.

Especially because he could be the other type of cut and paste guy—one who's just playing the numbers. He sends that message to every single woman who joins and is remotely attractive. He knows most women won't respond, but he gets a certain percentage that do, and if he works the numbers hard enough he occasionally gets a date and maybe even sex. He isn't interested in you as a person with unique wants and needs. You're just a faceless version of "woman" to him, interchangeable with all others. This is not the man you want to date seriously, let alone marry.

The scenario I gave you above is from one of the free sites. If you joined one of the pay sites this will be different. I don't recall as many married men on the personality profile sites— there might have still been one or two—and some of the more fringe interests don't show up there either. But you'll still get the cut and paste responses and hey hotties.

And you may still have twenty messages your first day, so be prepared for that. If you're especially attractive and have a fun and positive profile, it could be even more than that.

You're new blood and most men aren't shy about expressing interest, so every guy who is active on that site and saw your profile and found you interesting is going to reach out.

WHAT IF YOU DON'T GET RESPONSES?

I've tried online dating in my 20s and 30s and my experience has been that I had plenty of guys message me no matter my age or how snarky my profile. I tend to be vain, so I generally post a flattering photo, which might have something to do with it. But I would say that this is fairly common for all women who try online dating. I know it has been for my friends.

If for some reason you aren't getting a lot of messages, then I would have a trusted guy friend look at your photos and rate them from a guy's perspective. Only put up the ones that your guy friend gives his seal of approval. That may well fix the issue.

Also make sure that your profile and your photo are in synch. If you want fun, then have fun photos. If you want serious, nix the photos of you with a bunch of guys at a bar.

You may need to take pictures just for your dating profile. If so, do it. Grab a bottle of wine, a good camera, a few changes of clothes and have a good friend snap some realistic photos of you relaxed and enjoying yourself. Go for a hike if you need outdoorsy photos. Whatever it takes.

I'm convinced that pretty much anyone can take a flattering photo. It's just a question of how many bad photos you have to take before you get a good one. When I was eighteen I swear nine out of ten photos I took looked great. (Especially since that was in the film camera days and you only had so many chances to take a photo.) Now? Maybe one in forty looks good (thank God for digital cameras), but I can still get a good photo if I take enough of them. You can too.

If you don't have any good photos and don't want to ask a friend, sit down with a remote control and a video camera that lets you take photos and shoot a couple hundred of them. (That's how I got my blog photo.)

Seriously. Looks matter to men. And I swear that if you look beautiful in front of a man once he will store that image in his mind and view you through that lens until you give him a good reason to look beyond it. So, make sure you have at least one flattering photo up.

If that doesn't fix it, then it's time to think outside the box.

Be quirky. Be unique. Be bold. Be memorable.

Stand out from the crowd.

Everyone on these sites is trying to present themselves in the most flattering light, so what can you say that's real and genuine and will make a man stop and give you a shot?

I once admitted in a profile that I'm boring and like to spend my Friday nights at home watching TV. A number of guys messaged me about how different and refreshing that was. Maybe they were lying because of my profile photo, but maybe they meant it.

If you're not getting responses, what do you have to lose? Try it. (Not that, precisely, but something that makes you stand out from the crowd.)

YOU HAVE MESSAGES TO REPLY TO.
WHAT NOW?

Well, time to respond. Personally, any guy who does the one-liner message should just go in the delete bin. I also ignore the cut and paste guys. If a guy doesn't have time to write me a personal message, why should I spend my time writing him one?

But to each their own. You can write those guys, just don't expect it to get any better.

Think of it this way: this is supposed to be the time when a guy's putting his best foot forward in the effort to get your attention. He's supposed to be trying to impress you.

What you see right now may be the best he has to offer.

Scary thought, I know.

Eliminate the non-starters. Get to the ones that show some promise.

What next? Respond.

Easy enough, right?

No?

Okay then. What should you think about when you respond?

First, be yourself. I know the world of online dating is full of people who aren't being themselves, but if you want something real out of this, you need to be who you are from the start. Do you really want to fake who you are for the rest of your life? No. So don't do it now.

Be who you are. If a weird *Supernatural* reference pops into your head, include it. If you want to quote the latest Pitbull song, do so. Want to reference Debussy? Do it.

Second, remember that this is about attracting a man who is interested in you as a woman. So show your likeable, feminine side. That doesn't mean you can't insult a guy. I'm pretty good at the flirtatious dig and I couldn't be with a guy who couldn't take something like that and dish it back. And it doesn't mean you can't have opinions. Feel free to disagree with him if it's warranted.

But don't talk work or bring up all that career/education/ professional trajectory crap. If he asks one of those five-year plan questions, answer it, but then steer things back to the personal level.

Keep your messages focused on getting to know him and letting him get to know you as a person.

Think back to your best dates or most memorable conversations. What were those like? Fun, interesting, engaging? Do that.

Next thing you need to understand is that you probably aren't going to have a 100% success rate. As a matter of fact, I suspect that a few sites have phony profiles that they use to lure in new members.

Over the years I've received messages from guys that looked really promising. I'd see that I had a message waiting for me, join the site to message him back, and then never hear from him again.

Now, maybe I just put my foot in my mouth in that first message and the guy ran away. But I'm pretty good at those first few conversations, so it makes me wonder. Also, that really promising profile generally disappears only to be replaced with so-so matches.

Be forewarned. You will message guys back who seem promising and never hear from them again.

That's okay. Move on to the next one. Do not stake your hopes on just one guy.

What else should you do? Give him a reason to write back. See something in his profile and ask him about it. Or respond to his question and ask a follow-up question of your own.

Ask a question.

I've had guys message me that seemed somewhat interesting. Not fantastic, but somewhat interesting. So I responded and then they responded. But there was nothing in their response that required me to respond again. They just answered my question.

Since I had no real incentive to continue the conversation, I let it drop.

Don't let that happen to you. Give him a reason to continue the conversation. Ask a question. (Yes, I know I'm repeating myself. For a reason. Ask a question.)

I also tend to try to be complimentary and interested in him as an individual. (Also a good tactic when you meet in person.) I might ask where that picture was taken of him with the orphaned children and then respond how cool it is that he spent his summer after college volunteering in Angola and ask what that was like.

I also do try to share similar experiences if I have them. So, if I recognize a place, I might comment on it, like, "Is that Lake Atitlan, Guatemala? I went there years ago and loved it. What were you doing there?"

Find common interests.

Now is not the time to figure out if he earns enough to be a good provider or asking if he's saved enough for retirement. Make sure you like him first. And that he likes you.

Also, still protect your privacy. Don't tell him that you work at the Merrill Lynch office on H Street. Tell him you work downtown and are in financial services. Until you're sure of this guy, you don't need him being able to find you in the real world.

Paranoid, I know. But having seen what my potential matches are like on some of these sites and having had a pseudo stalker or two over the years, I'd rather be paranoid than trying to decide exactly when a guy has crossed the line into call the cops territory.

(And if he does cross that line, don't be shy about letting him know he has and shutting him down.)

Think of it this way, would you get on the subway and tell every man on there where you live and work? No? Then don't do it online either.

Now, while you're communicating you also need to be assessing this guy for more than just "are we compatible." You need to be looking for red flags that he is someone you need to avoid. Like what? Well...

RED FLAGS TO WATCH OUT FOR

What do I mean by red flags that a guy is someone to avoid? I mean you need to weed out the guys that no woman should date. Such as:

1. This is his first attempt at dating since he got divorced, ended a long-term relationship, or was widowed.

Two possible issues here.

First, he very well may be broken right now. If you enjoy fixing a man, great, but once he's fixed that's probably the end of your relationship, because co-dependency works for both parties and when he no longer needs to lean on you, you may not like him anymore.

If you want marriage and kids, skip the guy who needs fixing. Also, if you're looking for casual fun, this guy may start crying on your shoulder and want to cuddle instead.

Second, if he just went through an ugly breakup, he may hate women. He may claim to just hate his ex and call her a money-grubbing bitch or an out of control harlot or any of a number of other creative descriptions men seem to come up with for their exes.

And based on what he tells you, you may think he's right,

and that it's okay that he calls that woman those things, because, man, did she screw him over.

Here's my question for you: How long until you're that woman? What are you going to do that he doesn't like that's going to turn you from the love of his life into a hated foe?

Problem with men that carry that kind of anger towards women is that they don't tend to limit it to one woman. It's a pattern they form in their relationships and you don't want to get involved with a man like that.

You also don't know if what he's telling you is remotely close to the truth. Best to just avoid this type.

Which leads us into the second type of guy to avoid.

2. He has anger issues.

It may not be directed at you. It better not. He is trying to woo you after all. But he might let drop in conversation that he's pissed at his boss and hates the guy and just wants to fuckin' quit some days and then he got stuck behind this flippin' idiot on the highway who wouldn't know his ass from a hole in the ground and...

Look, we all have bad days. But don't date an angry man. You don't need that in your life. Anger is exhausting and draining. And men who carry a lot of anger in life, generally don't do so well in life. They get fired, they get in fights, they harm those they love, they have health issues from carrying those feelings around inside every day of their lives. None of that is worth it.

Which leads us to the third type of guy to avoid.

3. He has addiction or depression issues or is recovering from addiction or depression issues.

This one's trickier. I, personally, try to avoid men who have or have had addiction or depression issues. I don't think it's something you get over. I think it's something you manage to handle, but that means that you are never truly free of it.

Now, there are many wonderful people in this world who have overcome addictions or depression and are living perfectly happy, healthy lives. (My father was one.) There are also many people who have relapsed.

I want someone who can hold it together when the shit goes down—when we both lose our jobs and they're going to foreclose on the house and his mother is in the hospital and my brother is in a car accident. When that happens I want a guy who can keep it together and get through it, not someone who is quite likely to be facing the temptation to drink again or who spirals into a deep depression so I have to deal with him as well as everything else that's going wrong.

The hardest ones to spot are the ones that have a problem, but don't yet realize it. Where do you draw the line between someone who likes to go out and have fun and someone who has a drinking problem? Hard to tell sometimes. But if you're gut tells you there's something wrong, trust it and move on.

4. He's not what he seems.

Beware the man who comes on too strong. That's what a lot of serial cheaters and con men do. They spin you around so fast you can't even see straight.

Now, I've had that instant chemistry feeling, so it's hard sometimes to distinguish between someone you genuinely have a great connection with and someone who's playing you. But keep an eye out and don't trust everything without proof.

This man is a stranger to you.

You aren't dating your cousin's best friend here. You're meeting someone with no connection to you or your family or friends. They could be anyone. So just play it a little cool.

And don't agree to reship an unopened package for them or to loan them money.

Also, be alert to signs that maybe this guy isn't as single as he says he is. Does he only ever call from work? Is he only able to see you on short notice? Does he never want to have you over to his place? Some of those are only going to matter as you actually start dating, but keep it in mind at all stages. Not every guy online is legit.

CHECKING FOR COMPATIBILITY

So we've covered guys that no one should date. (In my opinion.) What about guys who aren't compatible with you?

This is a tough one. I think that many women, myself included, tend to be too picky. They want a man who has it all. Good job, incredibly fit, well-traveled, intelligent...blah, blah, blah. Ask most women what they want in a man and their list is twenty pages long. (I exaggerate. Slightly.)

I would encourage you, at least until after the first date, to be open to meeting men who don't fit your criteria. I'm not saying this has worked out for me, but I've enjoyed online dating more when I was open to meeting men that I wasn't sure would be good matches.

And if you are fixated on titles and certain professions and certain schools, reconsider. Personally, I think ambition, intelligence, and character matter more than what a man's résumé looks like.

One of my most compatible relationships was with a guy who never even went to college. There I was with my fancy degrees, but it didn't matter because what worked between us was that he was intelligent and driven to succeed. He just happened to have done so by joining the military. If I'd insisted on only dating doctors and lawyers and such I would've missed out on a great guy.

Now, having said that, I think there are certain reasons women set those standards. I have a friend who is a very accomplished professional. She busts her butt to succeed, which means long hours at work. We're talking sixty all the way up to a hundred plus each week.

She recently dated a guy who was happy to cruise through life. He worked forty hours and not a minute more. He wasn't the type to step up for an assignment or volunteer to go that extra mile. They couldn't have been more different in their approaches to life.

Not surprisingly, they didn't work out.

I'd encourage you to look past where a man is right now and instead think of who he is at his core and how that matches with you. Is he intelligent? Is he kind? Is he funny? Is he a hard-worker? Does he like animals? Does he like children? Is he active? Does he take risks?

Now, what you want him to be will be different from what I want my perfect match to be. If you don't particularly like kids, then you shouldn't choose a man who wants some of his own. Or, heaven forbid, already has some.

The key is to look past the obvious ways we judge people. You don't like his car? That can be changed. (Maybe, although it might be a symptom of how he approaches life. Me, I will never own a BMW or Mercedes for the sheer principle of the matter.)

I say this, but then again, maybe I have a bias. I want a man I'm compatible with on an emotional and intellectual level. Some women just want a man who can provide for them and if he brings home a big enough paycheck, that's enough. So be it. If that's all you want, then focus on that.

I'd just ask that you focus on the men who are also looking for something as limited in their relationship. They're out there and it can make a great long-term partnership. But if you find a man who wants a woman who's compatible on all levels and you only care about his income, it'll eventually destroy him and that's just not a nice thing to do to someone else.

Remember, even though this is online, you're still dealing with a human being on the other end of that computer.

Sorry, I digress. Back to the point: Look past the obvious criteria and give some guys a shot that you wouldn't otherwise.

SHOULD YOU MESSAGE GUYS FIRST?

You can. I know some guy friends who've been suitably impressed when it happened to them and they went on dates with the women in question.

It *will* make you stand out from the crowd, because there just aren't that many women who message men.

But.

And this is based on my real world experiences: Ask yourself why the guy didn't message you. He's on there to date, you're on there to date. Why didn't he reach out? Especially if you're tempted to message him because he in some way indicated that he liked your profile, so you know he saw you.

(I think certain sites send you different matches than they send the men, so it's not a guarantee that every guy you see has seen you.)

I've pursued men I liked in the real world. And I succeeded. But I also learned that it's not something I like to do. Why? Let me give you an example:

I met a guy at a party, had a great hour long conversation with him, and he didn't ask for my number when it was time for me to leave. Right before I walked out the door, I had a buddy of his give him my number. He called the next day and we dated for a few months. But there were reasons he didn't ask for my number and those are what ultimately ended that relationship. I was the one who kept things going as long as they did. If it was up to him, we would've fizzled out after a date or two. That's not a fun role to be in.

Another time I met a great guy during a random outing. We had an amazing connection, but he didn't ask for my number either. I reached out to him a month later and we still had a great connection. He remembered me and was glad to connect and flirt a bit.

Too bad he had a girlfriend.

See? He had a very good reason not to ask for my number.

Personally, I say don't do it. There are any number of reasons that a guy will respond if you reach out to him, but there's generally only one reason he will put himself on the line and reach out to you: Because he's interested.

So, do what you want. Just know that reaching out may not get you the result you want.

COMMUNICATING AWAY
FROM THE SITE

Messaging back and forth on the various sites is pretty easy. It's like any conversation, except via website.

But some men will ask you to communicate with them via e-mail or want to talk to you on the phone—especially on the paid sites. (I think some men sign up for a one-month membership and then try to get around the site by taking it offline.)

As before, you need to consider your privacy and safety. The nice thing about using an online dating site is that you can message with someone, decide you're not interested, and just end the conversation without having to deal with any sort of awkward follow-up e-mails, phone calls, or texts.

It's nice to avoid the backlash from the guy who was all nice and friendly until you say no and then decides to call you all sorts of nasty names and go on a rant about women.

If you take things to your personal e-mail account or give out your phone number, you may have to deal with that fallout.

I've given out my e-mail to a few guys I was going to meet up with or that I'd really hit it off with and it's been fine. I usually wait to give out a phone number until I've decided to meet someone for an actual date. That's just me.

I value my privacy and hate texting, so I don't see the point in giving a guy my number before he needs it. My friend willingly gives her number to guys as soon as they ask for it.

Just know that if you do give out your phone number, you may get random texts from the guy. Or he may just call you up to chat. If that's fine with you, then do it. If you know that it would annoy the hell out of you to get a call on a Thursday at 9 PM from a guy you've messaged with a few times, then don't.

Also know yourself. Will you turn annoying if you have the ability to text or e-mail him all the time? If so, don't do it. Don't open yourself up to being that woman.

If you are going to give out an e-mail address, think about setting up a new one just for dating. A friend of mine gave her e-mail to some guy and he friended her on Facebook before they'd ever even gone on a date because he used her e-mail to find her account.

So not cool.

Don't do that.

As with all of this, find where you're comfortable. Just remember that these sites are set up, in part, to provide you with a safe environment to meet someone. If you step outside of that environment, you are taking on additional risk. You have to if you really want to meet someone, just be smart about it.

SHUTTING A MATCH DOWN

Sometimes you'll communicate with a guy who seems promising, but it never seems to come together. He may be your most attractive match or your most interesting one or the only one of the bunch that likes karaoke. Whatever it is, you really like this guy.

But he isn't asking you out. He isn't trying to take it to the next level.

And maybe he disappears for days at a time. You message back and forth for a few days and then you don't hear from him for a week. Or two.

Sometimes he comes back with a legitimate excuse. (Sort of.) I had one guy say that he'd been biking in Italy and he didn't have good internet access and that's why he hadn't messaged me for two weeks.

Sounded legit. But I've traveled all over the world and haven't had an issue with internet access in probably the last eight to ten years. My smartphone works almost everywhere and I swear there are internet cafes in every town anymore. So, yeah.

In this connected world, it's really not true that a guy who wants to reach you can't do so in the space of two weeks. If that happens, it's a choice he's making. Other things in his life are more interesting or more important than reaching out to you.

Cut him loose and move on.

I know, he seems great. But chances are the guy has Plan B'ed you.

What is that? That's when a guy thinks you're somewhat interesting, but not as interesting as this other chick he's talking to. So he tries to string you along while he decides whether things with the other girl are going to work out. If they do, he disappears and you're left wondering what happened. If they don't, he turns his attention back to you until someone else new and shiny distracts him again.

You don't want to be with a guy who sees you as his second choice or his fallback plan. Move on and find a guy who thinks you're absolutely amazing.

WHEN TO MEET IN PERSON

So when should you go on a date with a guy you've met online?
Sooner is probably better than later.

I tend to drag things out a bit because I don't want to meet up with a guy who turns out to be a psycho. Another friend of mine was out on first dates within a few days of joining a site.

If you communicate for too long without meeting up in person, the conversation tends to die off after a while. The guy has other options and you do, too, so if you aren't immediately interested he'll look elsewhere.

I also had at least one situation where the guy got a little too cozy about our e-mails and was suggesting a first date curled up on the couch in his basement watching movies. And another where he started telling me about his back aches and pain medicines. You don't want to let the guy get too comfortable and you don't want to get too comfortable either.

Also, if you let the messaging back and forth go on for too long you may get so tied up with what you think this guy is that you fail to see who he really is. A man can take as long as he wants to compose a message to you online. He can even have his friends review it. Hell, he can have his friends write it.

The only way to know who he really is, is to meet him in person.

If you're interested, get together. Make sure that his pictures and his in-person-persona match as soon as you can.

Remember, people do lie. For all you know, everything you see in that profile is bullshit. And even if it isn't, there's this thing called in-person chemistry that matters more than most of us are willing to admit. A guy can seem great online and then you meet him in real life and it falls flat.

So exchange a few messages to make sure he's not insane and then agree to meet up.

It's okay. That's the point, right?

BE SAFE

Don't let the fact that this guy seems fantastic blind you to the fact that you're meeting a complete stranger for the first time.

What should you do to be safe on that first date?

1. Meet him somewhere public.

Don't have him come to your house. Don't go to his. Don't agree to meet at the end of some remote trailhead for a hike.

2. Choose a date that allows either one of you to leave with ease.

Don't go on a boat cruise. Don't agree to go for a drive in his fancy convertible. Don't fly to another city in his private jet. (Sounds fun until you're stuck somewhere remote with a guy who expects certain things before you can go home.)

3. Watch your alcohol or drug use.

We each have our personal limits on this, but this is a stranger, and it might behoove you to stay aware of your surroundings and what's happening.

* * *

Those are the biggies. You can also tell someone you know where you're going and what his name is and what site you met him on and maybe give them his contact information if you have it. Personally, I tend to be more private than that and wouldn't tell anyone those kind of details. If I go missing, they can find it on my computer.

(By then it's already too late anyway.)

I do generally tell my family or friends that I have a date just because it comes up in conversation, not for safety.

The key here is to acknowledge that online dating is different from dating in the real world. If you meet someone in real life and he asks you out, you've already met him. You've already determined that he doesn't exhibit any of those warning signs that make a guy instantly creepy. But with online dating, you haven't had that chance yet.

Most men give themselves away with their profile or their messages and you'll probably be able to avoid the worst, but there will still be some that slip through. And you don't want to be sitting in your living room, three sheets to the wind, when it occurs to you that you're on a date with a psychopath.

So play the first date safe. Or at least the first three hours of the first date safe.

If you make it through three hours and it's going well and you haven't seen any warning signs, then let the date go where it may. But start off in a safe space.

Especially, especially, if this is a "just for fun" situation. I'm not really that girl, so I can't give good advice here, but if you're used to hooking up with guys at college parties, online dating is different. Colleges are sort of a pre-screened population. Online dating is not. And if you go looking for sex, you will find it, but you may also find guys not willing to let you say no or not willing to respect your limits.

I had a friend who met a number of guys online for sex and enjoyed the experience quite a bit. But she also told me a story about one of those guys and how he choked her during sex the first time they were together. Now, that worked for her and she really enjoyed it.

Me, if I met up with a stranger and the first time we had sex he decided to choke me without getting my permission first, I think I'd panic and feel like I was in a very dangerous situation. That man would lose vital parts of his anatomy.

I don't want to sound like anyone's mother, but be safe, please.

Speaking of, let's talk sex.

SEX

You met someone online, you've hit it off, and now…You want to have sex.

First, think about your sexual safety. I'm not your mom, but I'm going to act like it for a minute. If you're going into online dating and you don't have strong moral or religious reasons for waiting to have sex, chances are that will be on the table at some point. Think about it now before you get started.

Do you have condoms?

Personally, I think the guy should have them. But …if I get myself into a hot and heavy situation where I want things to happen, I'd rather have some on hand than make a stupid choice to go without or have to wait while he makes a run to the store.

So stock up on some condoms. Five bucks well-spent just in case.

Now, maybe you don't like condoms. Maybe you don't want to ask a guy to wear one. (Why you're having sex with a man you can't communicate with, we won't get into, but think about that a bit.)

If you're not using condoms, how are you protecting yourself from sexually-transmitted diseases? (Or is it sexually-transmitted infections these days? I'm showing my age, aren't I?)

Whatever you call them, STDs or STIs, how are you ensuring that you don't walk away from this experience with herpes or crabs or syphilis or whatever else is out there?

Condoms are very helpful in that respect. If you don't go the condom route, then maybe you go the testing route and you both get tested before you have sex.

Of course, that route presupposes that neither one of you are currently sexually active with other partners. Do you know that about him? Have you asked?

Do not assume that you know the answer to that question.

And ask yourself if you're positive that he's telling you the truth. Make a mistake on this and you may have a life-time to remember him.

The second thing you need to think about is pregnancy. Maybe you're already on birth control and have been forever and it's all good. If you're not, most birth control methods require time between when you start taking them and when you can have sex.

And most require a visit to the doctor to get started.

With birth control pills you need to wait until the end of your cycle and start taking them and then they aren't really effective for about a month after that. Something like an IUD needs to be inserted by the doctor, which means waiting for the appointment, and then you have to wait a few more days until you can have sex.

Again, condoms can be a good choice for when you haven't arranged something else, but best to think of this now and get it lined up before you're in the heat of the moment and tempted to let a guy try the pull out method.

And stick to your guns. If you want a guy to use a condom, then insist he do so. If you know you can't safely have sex until Tuesday because you had an IUD put in yesterday, then don't let him badger you into having sex today.

My best advice is to go into each date knowing what you're willing to have happen. It's a helluva lot easier to start out a night sober and unaffected by the situation and say, "I'm only comfortable fooling around. It's too early in our relationship to have sex" than to try to figure out exactly what you're willing to have happen while it's happening. In my experience, if you wait until that moment you end up doing more than you'd planned for. So plan ahead.

And, no, you are never too old to have to think about these things. I don't know where I saw it, but the 60+ age range is at the top for acquiring STDs. It's great to have fun. Just be safe about it.

WHEN TO HAVE SEX

So when should you have sex with someone you meet online? Whenever you're comfortable doing so.

Now, having said that, and acknowledging that each relationship is different, in general, if you are looking for a long-term relationship, you should probably wait a few dates to have sex. Maybe even more than a few dates.

No matter that it takes two to have sex and that if you sleep with a guy on the first date he also slept with you on the first date, you risk flipping that little switch in a guy's head where he just views you as someone to have sex with but nothing more than that. And you two might have a great time together for a bit, but sex clouds the brain.

And it doesn't just cloud a man's brain, it clouds yours, too. When the sex is great it's easy to overlook all the ways you guys aren't compatible. All the little deal-breakers that are going to prevent this relationship from continuing exist, but if you're in that heady glow from good sex, you'll gloss right over them.

So, as 50's housewife as it sounds, I say hold off a bit.

My personal experience is that most men are trying to have sex with me for the first three dates. If I get past that and we haven't had sex I finally get to see what they're genuinely like and what they actually think about me.

Now, having said that. I also don't believe in artificially stopping something that's progressing well. So don't destroy a potential relationship by setting some arbitrary limits on yourself.

Again, do what you're comfortable with when you're comfortable with it.

THE FIRST DATE

Here I went and talked about sex and we haven't even talked about the first date yet. I know this is a book about online dating, but there are a few weird things that happen with a first date that started out with online dating that you may not expect.

Primary one is this: men will ask you to go for coffee or a drink more times than they'll ask you to do anything else.

Personally, I hate this. Because if a guy asks you for a drink, he's usually not actually asking you for a drink. He's testing you out to see if you're worth him spending the money for dinner.

So what happens is you meet up for a drink. It goes well and he casually says, "Do you want to grab something to eat?" and you end up having dinner. It annoys the shit out of me, because I pass the drink test nine times out of ten.

But that's the reality of online dating. Men go on a lot more dates because they can't be sure until they meet you whether it's going to click or not. Which makes them cheap and cautious to commit to too much time together.

(You may get that way, too, someday and be pleased that it's only a coffee or drink date. Honestly, the last date I went on was a dinner date and I would've been fine with that just being a drink date.)

Be prepared for that. If you can, try to suggest an activity date instead. They tend to be much more fun and help with the nerves.

Also, expect to pay. Now, I think I've only had to pay for a couple of dates over the years, but I walk into every one expecting to have to pay for it. And offering to pay when the check comes. Most men are gentlemanly about it and wave me off, but there are those few that let the check sit and sit and sit on the table because they don't want to pay for it. In my experience, it happens more with online dating than dating someone you meet in the real world.

Your best bet is to go into each date assuming you're paying for it and then be pleasantly surprised and thank the man when he says he's got it.

And do thank him. This is a two-way street. He does something nice like gets the door, say thank you. Or compliments you, say thank you.

(Although I've shut down a few matches because the guy was just too too over the top with compliments when we were communicating online. Made me wonder why he felt this constant need to compliment rather than connect, but that's me and I'm weird. YMMV.)

CONCLUSION

That's about it. I've told you everything I can think of to help you get started. Let's see if we can't rehash it:

1. Be honest with yourself about what you want.

2. Be honest with others about what you want.

3. Be patient and persistent.

4. Be open to meeting men that aren't what you think you want.

5. Pick the right site or app for what you're looking for.

6. Remember these guys are complete strangers and may lie.

7. Align your user name/photos/profile with what you want.

8. Remember that you're dating, so be womanly not professional.

9. Unless you just want fun, be attractive but not too sexy.

10. Be yourself.

11. Avoid men who are damaged.

12. Be safe (sexually and otherwise).

And, last, but not least, have fun with it. Worst case scenario, you end up with some great stories to tell the girls over drinks. (Assuming you followed my advice and were safe.) Best case scenario, you meet the guy you're looking for and you happily whatever it was you wanted for as long as you wanted it to last.

Good luck.

ABOUT THE AUTHOR

Cassie Leigh is a bit like the jaded older sister you never had. She's been there done that and can help you navigate the crazy world of online dating so you hopefully walk away the happy half of a couple instead of a lonely old woman like her. (Haha…)

www.ingramcontent.com/pod-product-compliance
Lightning Source LLC
Chambersburg PA
CBHW071240020426
42333CB00015B/1559